T0067221

POETRY

The Four Lives

Nicholas Pak

BALBOA.
PRESS
A DIVISION OF HAY HOUSE

Balboa Press books may be ordered through booksellers or by contacting:

Balboa Press
A Division of Hay House
1663 Liberty Drive
Bloomington, IN 47403
www.balboapress.com.au
1 (877) 407-4847

Because of the dynamic nature of the Internet, any web addresses or links contained in this book may have changed since publication and may no longer be valid. The views expressed in this work are solely those of the author and do not necessarily reflect the views of the publisher, and the publisher hereby disclaims any responsibility for them.

The author of this book does not dispense medical advice or prescribe the use of any technique as a form of treatment for physical, emotional, or medical problems without the advice of a physician, either directly or indirectly. The intent of the author is only to offer information of a general nature to help you in your quest for emotional and spiritual well-being. In the event you use any of the information in this book for yourself, which is your constitutional right, the author and the publisher assume no responsibility for your actions.

Any people depicted in stock imagery provided by Thinkstock are models, and such images are being used for illustrative purposes only.
Certain stock imagery © Thinkstock.

Print information available on the last page.

ISBN: 978-1-5043-1036-9 (sc)
ISBN: 978-1-5043-1037-6 (e)

Balboa Press rev. date: 09/22/2017

Dedicated to all whose lives I had the privilege to observe or share.

CONTENTS

THE FOUR LIVES

With spring, there comes
Light and life anew
Blues and pinks
Adventure to the few
Flowers spring forth
Open arms to the sun
Colours abound
We watch them run
As spring turns to summer
Trunks sprout tall
Strong as an ox
All others in there thrall
Sunlight shines
A warm embrace
Branches grow strong
Everything in its place
But always autumn
Hard on its heels
Leaves come falling
An emotional reel
Green becomes brown
From luscious to dry
Soon the ride ends
And we will all lie
Winter now inevitable
Night shrouds the sky
We stare at the stars
And gasp with a sigh
The cold sets in
One last moon beam
Each says their goodbyes
Its time now to dream.

THE VIKING

I hath not seen thou
For years, on end
And will, nevermore
My long lost friend

A Viking, of the road
Thou set out to be
Yet found, something more
Your own, family

A fate, premature
Closed, on your heel
Some country road
It doth not seem real

Your breath, escaped
No-one, informed me so
No chance to mourn thee
These feelings of sorrow

Grass, now grows
Where the dirt, was thrown
Flowers and respects
I wish I had known

Now you float on clouds
And watch over your kin
Twinkling in the sky
Is how I'll remember him.

LEGEND

Teens taken before their time,
Heroes struck down in their prime.
Why do the brightest burn out,
So Fast?
How is it, their memories, seem to last?
Bruce, the dragon,
Death by misadventure.
Brandon, the son,
Side by side, the sepulture.
Jimmy Dean, a star on the rise,
His legend cemented, upon his demise.
Hendrix exploded, one in a jillion,
Music transcendent, his life a tourbillion.
Imagine John Lennon, proponent of peace,
Pierced on his doorstep, in a heartbeat,
Ceased.
River drank deep, from an empty cup,
Became his undoing, no more than a pup.
Cobain caught the train, though, all in all,
Captured our souls, before a great fall.
Each one, though passed, their myth,
Forever present.
Their lights in our hearts, and with,
Our descent.
Still with the power, to make us rise,
They will continue to do so,
When the future arrives.

BETTER DAYS

Lovers, haters and motivators
All with their wishes
Make up our lives
Drive us onward
Towards our fate
No revelation
Ever comes too late
Hitch up your britches
And steel yourself
Life is for living
Don't waste yourself
When revolution comes
Jump that train
In sickness or good health
Soak up the rain
What you don't know
Do not despise
There is no need
For secrets and lies
Turn to the sun
And embrace its rays
Soon there will come
Better days.

MUSINGS OF HER

What is her smile worth?
A rainbow after a storm
When I feel I've been inearthed
When I am feeling forlorn

How do I value her compassion?
A warm summer breeze
Washing over me when I'm ashen

What is the limit of her generosity?
I shall compare it, with time infinite
Is it real? Can she really be?

How do I repay her faith in me?
By devoting myself with loyalty
Her strength gives me the courage I need

How do I measure her love?
With God's forgiveness
As pure as a dove

What does her kindness mean to me?
Her heart, deep as the ocean,
Is all I need to see

How much do I need her?
As much as flowers need the sun

Without her, what would I be?
A mess of vulnerability.

What would I do without her?
Drift aimlessly?

THE DEVIL SAYS HELLO

Be careful when you sink into bliss
That it doesn't become the final kiss
Silence is the only sound
Darkness the colour that I found
A derma of pale, a roll of the dice
No breath passes
Between lips of blue ice
Your mind floats on clouds
Engulfed in a shroud
But your body lies lifeless
Heavy, despite being soulless
The hammer flows, while,
Fists hammer your chest
Water splashes
Make haste, lest.....
Then something stirs
Consciousness beckons
The smell of alcohol, pinpricks,
The rush of narcaine
Eyes open wide, focus, look around
Unfamiliar faces stare and crowd
Then the feeling hits
Nausea and convulsions
Adrenaline counters slowness
A sickening concoction
Senses are regained
Realization sets in
You've dodged a bullet
The Devil's kiss.

(Time) Release Or Peace

Bright light shines,
In my pupils,
Pinned,
To the ground,
Yet floating on cloud,
9.
Triptomaniac.
Fill the void with,
Lonely,
Emptiness.
Replace your soul,
With a worn out,
Hole.
Taste the taste.
Smell the,
Alcohol.
Hold back the,
Flow.
White night.
Red is,
Dead.
Control the,
Fit.
Release the,
Brick.
But, time to find the,
Time.
We must do. Find,
Peace.
Or, at least,
Release.

REASONS

You can't call me an iconoclast
For then I'd have to have reasons
Reasons for disbelieving
And then I'd have reasons
For something else to believe in
But words mean nothing
Think otherwise and you're dreaming
I'd rather be a crying freeman
Still, there's no need for grieving
We don't have to worry about treason
But he is universal
Don't take it as a reversal
That's not what I'm disagreeing…..
It's religion which causes division
So what am I to do?
That's for me to choose
I'm not preaching to you
We both know you're no fool
You and I both, may decide
To go our own way, in life
If that's how it has to be
Then don't shed a tear for me
In the end we're essentially the same
The same, sane, but insane
Take that candle and hold it to the sky
Humans weren't meant to fly
All I want is to live before I die
That's why we go on, why we try
I respect that you have your faith
We all want to keep our spirits safe
My destiny, I'll leave in God's hands
And just try to do the best that I can.

Shadow's Road

You don't think you'll lose control
When you start out on that stroll
The end of the road is clouded with doubt
And shadows loom right throughout
And the trees block your view of the woods
Buried within is your sense of what's good
Everything, seems alright
But you're heading toward everlasting night
Years go by, one thing leads to another
With age you degrade and you'd sell your own mother
The wear and tear and scars you bare
Are yours alone cause nobody cares
It's been so long since you knew who you were
Emotionally stunted, you've forgotten about her
Some you lose along the way
As you lose yourself, at the end of the day
Maybe you'll be able to find your way back
Despite the numbers and time you lack
How some make it when most don't
Is a mystery of the wont
Make sure you don't exchange your pain
There's no one else for you to blame
Take control before you turn black
You don't need to use that track
Believe me, there's no excuse
That's just a spiraling cycle of abuse
If you take it from one day to the next
Moving on with your life is not that complex
I've stood out there in the rain
Changed my game, gone through the same
I know that path is one of hurt
But everyone knows what its worth.

BLEED

What time marks
Things that last
Memories and circumstance
Leave behind the past;
When automatic are your thoughts
To train them you must resort,
My mind so sublime
When refrained from lapsed time
When flows like a rhyme
Self-betrayal my crime;
Attention to detail
Is why I always fail
Holding on for too long
Destroys the soul of the song
Stop to pause, then let roll
With the water I loll
Contained in each cup
Allowed to crash and erupt;
Sentiment still lingers, but
Broken are my fingers,
Making it hard to reach, touch,
Like modern life, things are such
Striving for meaning, yet naught
Between walls I am caught
Huddling for warmth
The shadows are staunch
On the inside of out
Passing forebears doubt
How to register my name?
Do away with blame, and

Weigh the risks. Grace
Is overrated. How would you
Know you have made it?
If not for what's known
My mirror has shown,
All that's left is to bleed,
Bandage and take heed.

Fated Cross

Dare
To bear
The scars
Of past;
Reveal them now, or
Forever they will last.
Take the time
To open your mind,
Forgiveness they say
Will save the day;
If it's true,
I don't know;
Ask the few,
They claim so;
I try, but
Find it too much,
I strive, but
Still need a crutch;
Over and over
I create,
Lower and lower
My cross of fate;
I want to carry it
Up that hill,
Nail myself to it
And get my fill;
Depressing it sounds
I understand,
But this, I've found
Is at least not bland.

For Open Souls

Wonder went, out of mind
When exchanged, were glasses, of different kind
As I learnt, to mull on such
Replaced the light, for the rush
Would cope with hope, be displaced?
If I had a smile upon my face
Way too far, that distant day
For my heart, with truth to say
From standing tall, on two firm feet
To broken doors, cut at the knees
This turn in fortune, was not meant
Now I yearn, with no event
I wish there was a way to trade
Without losing lessons, with pain I've made
This life, I fear, is at an end
Though they say, with time, I'll mend
Do I believe, what's writ is wrote
Or wait with patience, the changing note
Every day I hope for more
Can't explain why I glow no more
I chew on glass and bleed disease
Smoke cigarettes, choke and wheeze
Like the lion that didn't roar
The eagle tried but couldn't soar
Cold is heart, is hard to find
But bitter fritters, no use to whine
Just you is no use, one half a pair
Keep on my search, she'll be somewhere
Existence isn't, how meant to see
One day I'll say, receive sincerely
If not now, when tomorrow comes
For open souls, when all's said and done.

THE WAY

Black and white, not opposites
As they would seem
But flow into each other
As if in a dream
Flexible as bamboo
Formless like water
Take any direction
Method in disorder
The universe is chaos
Energy undying
We are the stars
All of us flying
Unrestricted mind
Unlimited limit
Circle without circumference
Every change in a minute
The dragon swoops
Signals his lover with fire
The phoenix rises
No longer burning on its pyre.

TWILIGHT

Old and grey and withered away,
The sun has gone down on another day.
Together we were,
when it began.
When night comes around,
only one of us shall stand.
There was a time,
when we were inseparable.
But now only God,
may prevent the insufferable.
When we were young,
the sky was the limit.
But now that I'm old,
I have grown timid.
Looking through, your sweet eyes,
I can see your warmth clearly.
Although, I can tell,
that you've become weary.
You're the one person,
I can't stand to mourn.
So I pray, to the Lord,
you'll make it to dawn
But time is infinite,
unless you are human.
You weaken each minute,
and death is soon looming.
My love is now dwindling,
I hear the last rites.
Once more, I find your eyes,

but this time no lights.
The dust will soon settle,
and I will go on.
But life is now empty,
and I don't know for how long.

RENDEZVOUS

It was dusk in the village
where this story takes place
The young man skipped to his lover
with a smile upon his face
For tonight they would steal away
into the night
But little did they know
for their love, they'd have to fight
They met by the light
of an old oil street lamp
The streets were all foggy
and the grass was damp
As she approached
his stomach felt hollow
In the dark distance
a stranger did follow
They closed on each other
fell into embrace
She looked at him lovingly
but something crossed his face
Looking back from whence she came
a figure emerged
They both stood still, frozen,
as one their hearts surged
The face became clear
that of, a jealous suitor
A shot rang out
as loud as a hooter
The girl leapt in front
of the one she adored
And they lost in an instant

what neither could afford
The two rivals stared
for what seemed like an age
Then the destroyer of love
disappeared from the stage
The young lover looked
at the gun on the ground
And did the one thing he could
with the last round.

THE TWO HEAVENS SWORD

The sun glared down
upon the green field
These two fierce warriors
have no use for a shield
Their eyes fixed forward
a piercing stare
Across from each other
they stood square to square
As quick as a falcon
they both broke the gaze
Swords were soon whirling
as if in a haze
These soldiers of fortune
as ronin, they were known
Once were great samurai
but now free to roam
Their lords long since dead
legend they sought
Slicing and thrusting
with grim defiance they fought
Musashi, the senior
a sword in each hand
A hero to many
no equal in the land
The younger was fast
agile and quick
To any onlooker
the old man looked sick
But he was a fox
luring his foe into a trap
Soon he would show

why he's known throughout the map
He faked left and right
up and then down
Then there was a head
rolling along the ground
The victor stood tall
his blade stained red
Tonight he would sleep sound
no burden in his head
For he was Musashi
the Two Heavens Sword
The Book of Five Rings
He needed no lord.

THE VICIOUS CYCLE

The night was restless
tossing and turning
He had aches and pains
his veins were burning
What kept him going
on through the night
Was the taste he'd receive
at the break of first light
He stretched out his muscles
splashed water on his face
Get money quickly
that was the case
He ran down the stairs
and out the front door
The sun on his face
the wind chilled him to the core
He made it to the bank
as if he was made out of sticks
Then on to the flats
to find his first fix
With each step he took
the worse it seemed to be
But he would find his relief
and set himself free
The candy man stood there
beneath a palm tree
A smile on his dial
the goods for him to see
Without hesitation
he picked up his gear
Then charged to a building

and went 'round the rear
It took only minutes
to find the old place
And give him release
into the right space
No other feeling
could rival this kind
No other comfort
could ease his ill mind
Back to his cave
to nod in his lair
The journey was peaceful
as warm as summer air
He went back inside
through the front door
To start over again
and hang out once more.

TORMENT

He knew no memories
'ccept the love of his wife
Which no man could alter
nor surgeon's knife
Once he was a giant
of intellectual pursuit
Now walking darkness
the void, he'd been reduced
Too damaged to remember
conscious to realize
Plunged into the vastness
of the pits of Hell's fires
Each agony he awaited
the amnesiac's torments
Their rendezvous he would forget
in a matter of mere moments
Through the tears he cried
the inability to speak
One thing remained
the love he would seek
Each day anew
the life he couldn't recall
The words "I love you"
and the name he would call.

Rebirth

An oasis in the middle
no shelter from the rain
To the one who would pace
fucking circles he'd exclaim
On the perimeter they would sit
and light up their fires
From the corner of his eyes
paranoid of the liars
But time passed by
no longer needing his mask
He opened his chest
life was his task
No hostiles around
a friend on each side
A sanctuary he'd found
no need to hide.

THE MACAW

Deep in the Amazon,
Far from the jungle floor.
He gazed upon the beauty,
Of the rainbow macaw.

It rode on the wind,
Its colours fluorescent.
As it made its way down,
To its descent.

It circled its way down,
From canopy height.
A picture of perfection,
Mother Nature's delight.

HOMECOMING

Twenty-one days in winter
The cold and an empty stare
Every Friday the treatment
A disease all too rare
A derelict fountain, in the middle
Enclosed, by walls around
Cancer sticks, would fill their lungs
Ears tuned, to the music's sound
From dawn 'till dusk, every moment
In her body, aches and pain
This body, it seems, a lifetime ago
Once proud, but now her bane
Ravaged by the incurable
Meditation to ease the mind
But light shines down, evermore
And God is by her side
The seasons change, once again
And spring, blooms its way through
Fear subsides, the love of those close
And hope begins anew
Now is the time of homecoming
A time for all to rejoice
There is comfort found, in her heart
When night falls, she finds her voice.

BEAUTY INCOMPARABLE

She had a beauty beyond compare
A sight to behold
The body of a ballerina
A face as precious as gold
Her voice was like an angel's
Her laughter danced upon the air
Eyes of emerald green
Skin like silk and fair
A touch which shook the strongest knees
Made transparent by her gaze
Her lips would pout, soft as pillows
Mesmerized by her ways
Her hair so soft
Her perfume so sweet
Her mind was like a maze
A woman of such uniqueness
All others, mortally mere
A blessing to those on the outside
Those within she held so dear.

THE DIVINE WIND

The grandfather had built an empire
The grandson stretched it further
But one thing remained, to seal his greatness
The land of Nippon required much murder
A fleet set sail in 1281
Forty-four hundred strong
They arrived off the shores of Takashima
But something would go disastrously wrong
Feared by reputation
The Mongol hordes without mercy
But they were men of horseback
And knew nothing of the high sea
Their challenge, they thought, were samurai
Great warriors in their own right
Except they were not the enemy
For their lives, they'd have to fight
Only one battle, would these two tribes
Meet upon the field
The Mongols forced, into retreat
Still neither army would yield
The invaders fell, back to their ships
And decided to bide their time
But before they could mount, another attack
On the horizon, something would rise
The Nipponese had prayed for a kamikaze
A divine wind, to protect their home
This super typhoon came at their bidding
And the empire would go the way of Rome
But the mistake was made by the emperor
When all of this began

The fleet was comprised of river boats
They keeled over, and the hordes were damned
Their leader had been impatient
He lost his myth, and right arm
Over 70,000 men
Spelled the end, of Kublai Khan

PSYCHOSIS

Sitting and thinking
Alone with my thoughts
Discuss your feelings
Electric shocks
A break with reality
And perception
Submitted for
Psychological testing
Disorganised thoughts
I can hear their sound
The tree forms clouds
Not the other way 'round
Induced psychosis
Paranoia strikes
Scheduled and locked
Know your rights
Poked and prodded
Analyzed and worked out
Tested and rearranged
I need to shout
CBT and medication
The dawn of meaning
Into remission
You win your freedom.

IRONY

The sociopath hunts at night
Stalking his vulnerable prey
A smile etched across his face
Inviting her in to stay
His tongue was, as smooth as silk
A sling around one arm
Look beneath, his cold steel eyes
There's something more than charm
The victim comes in, unaware
In his mind he rubs his hands
But there's more to this lass, than he can see
He doesn't know where he stands
The door closes behind them
The predator turns up the music
He pulls his knife, and turns around
But he's stabbed before he can use it
He falls to the ground, blood pours out
And looks up in disbelief
She is his match, in every shape
This wolf, hardly a sheep
She steps, over him, wipes her knife
Empties out his wallet
Adding insult to injury, she disappears through the door
And takes everything worth a dollar.

Love And Attraction

Their love was entrancing
A thing of mystery
What pulls two lovers together?
A magnetic gravity

Enticed by shape and form
Brought closer by chemistry
Sealed by, one first kiss
A magic memory

Two minds made, for each other
Their hearts, complementary
A love to last, through the ages
Compatible, personalities

The passion of youth
The commitment of family
Desire which never fades
Their fires burn bright
Grow old with faith
The wisdom which comes from age

A partnership, unfathomable
Love, which will never die
When these two, are made dust
They'll continue to light up the sky.

In The Groove

Flow like a river
Kick back, no disdain
Fly like a comet
Exerting no pain
We are unbound
Following the goliards
Swinging with the sounds
We are all love's shepherds
Angels from heaven
Slicing holes in night's curtain
What to do is decided
Mentalities made certain
Trapped, we are, no longer
Every word a confession
Freedom found in our art
Sessions release the repression
Not chained by believing
Uncommitted to the cause
Passed jaded and disbelieving
Every moment, offers pause
Smell the sweet fragrance
Float on the wind
Chant with infinite patience
Bereft of man's sins.

THE GIANTS

Plato came and opened our minds
Aristotle, took us further
Metaphysics written, with passion
Words of ancient furore
Confucius, revered, through the ages
Sun Tzu's Art of War
The Tao's balance, of the stages
The grace, of the I-Ching's open door
Da Vinci, master of renaissance
Michelangelo's cistine chapel
Newton, a giant of his time
With great ideas, he would grapple
Descartes, trod, a dangerous path
Many took, that ultimate fall
Darwin sowed, a plentiful seed
Evolution changed us all
Shakespeare's works, art defined
Still played out to this day
Oscar Wilde, a rampaging wit
His mind knew no other way
Nietzsche conceived, the Ubermensch
Before he could write no more
Nihilism plagued his existence
He was struck down, to his core
Freud was an original
Jung followed his lead
But time shifts sand, and our thoughts
And he would find, his own ideals
Edison brought, a revolution
Electricity, for the masses

But the king of the giants was Einstein
His Unified Field caused him hassles
Despite this, the Theory of Relativity
E=mc squared
He was the first to split the atom
With genius, his name was paired.

THE DARK HORSE

Through the blackened forest
Escaping trees, and obstacles, in between
The sinking earth, which swallows
Exerts his muscles, becomes lean

Leaving behind, the darkness and gloom
Branches and vines, which claw
Out and over and over
He discovers, the rolling moor

Strives to the peaks, and breathes
Continues on the run
The valley, he finds, runs deep
His lover, signals to come

In the sun, his body glitters
Demons, no more, on his tail
Candlelight, in the chateau, flickers
A mission, he cannot fail.

EPIPHANY

Two lovers, could not be more
Out of touch and far
Struggling to understand
A love, no less than bizarre

He looked at her
With accusatory windows
Unblinking and without guilt
She mirrored the pose

Then, suddenly, his expression shifted
In her, was something, he had not seen before
A well of emotion, below the surface
Reaching out, he enveloped her, and was sure

Curled together, like two cats
They wept, for their wasted time
Fears, now amounted, to nothingness
Their souls, part of one rhyme

In her eyes, now, sweet sorrow
His, unmistakable
Huddled, from moonlight to light break
Shivering, this epiphany, unfakeable

Nevermore, apart in spirit
Union, made concrete
Bliss, in realization
No longer, at her feet.

CHAINED SOULS

O special friend
O special stranger
How oft have we met?
How oft do we endanger?

Turning, to the slow one
Sinking, into bliss
Finding, misery
Chasing, that kiss

Years, we apart
Still, the taunting
Upon, each reunion
The demons, haunting

Mine, faceless
Yours, much too near
An everlasting companion
Brought here by fear

The past taps, on our shoulders
How we did not disappear
Thou art still struggling
I have changed gear

O special friend
O special stranger
We will meet again
Leave behind your manger.

INSPIRATION

O words, and words, of,
Old country and mine
How resplendent it is
To arrange and rhyme

The ways of the poet
Passed from humble beginnings
Such passion and atmosphere
Their words, underpinning

Verse of the masters
Edgar Allan Poe
Blake and Wordsworth
Built, to crescendo

This one an ode
To those of the past
Magnificence, undying
Their memories will last.

Vagabond

The vagabond strolls
Through town, and wonders
Who are the nameless?
The many floribundas

Each mask, he surveys
The cold, the enchanting
Zigzagging in haste
On the corner, ranting

Time was, he an ant
A penguin with an agenda
Now, a different slant
No more, a pretender

Taking in its soul
Colours and noise
Amongst the pillars
First of his joys

Coming, upon
The shimmering blue
He casts down
A reflecting pool

In it, he sees
A grisly picture
In shock, takes one last breath
And jumps, in the river.

JOURNEY SOMEWISE

Bright and joyful, after the sunder
Days went slow, full of wonder
Every adventure, impressed like thunder
But soon they would be, torn asunder

Those held close, to my heart
Became memories, when they did part
Pierced my chest, like a dart
My mission became, each new sweetheart

Butterflies, which came to me
Never stayed, to really see
Betrayed by myself, decided to flee
Youth does not know, it's temporary

Searching for, the dark robed one
Eluding him, he would not come
Dancing through the night, shun the sun
No longer finding, the suffusion fun

Emerging from, the chilly bleakness
Look behind, see the weakness
Without thrall, life glows, kissless
Forget, insanity, and its weirdness

Now the next, what shall rise?
In her eyes, she does not despise
At journey's end, will there be a prize?
A floating city or just somewise?

THE FORUM

As the people, bustle, and shuffle,
Along, the forum lives, and sings its song
But come weeks end, and Sunday morn'
It dies a death, the wind blows strong

The shops close their shutters,
Board up their doors
Only the station, awake
Beneath the floors

The dream chasers, alone
Haunt the empty strip
Taken, their daily sugar
Rocks and pinpricks in their grip

They mingle, and linger
Spout, their tortured thoughts
Harassed, by the blue men
For hustles, and rorts

Day turns to night
Night into day
Life starts again
Death walkers, blown away

The daystar, blazes down
A musician strums with his plectrum
Cockalorums mill about, the
Forum's revolving spectrum.

ANGUISH

Can they hear me?
Can they read me?
Are they watching? Or,
Is it just me?

Is my anguish, all,
For naught?
My mind distraught.
A deafening squall.

Whispers, I hear.
Words, of degradation.
My searing ear.
Give me elucidation.

Should I fight or flee?
This is not me.
Senses overwrought.
Where's the peace I've sought?

I turn, to the night sky.
A silent plea.
It smiles at me.
I ask the moon, why?

Do I have, the wherewithal,
To find, my emancipation?
Will I be, forever in thrall,
From cognitive, anticipation?

Is my grief announced?
Have I been denounced?

CORUSCATION

Simple souls, find hope,
In everything they survey.
Which of them, will use the rope,
Or nepenthes, can we spae?

What sanguine expectations, should,
The starry-eyed possess?
Youthfuls, often, misunderstood,
For debauchery, unless... ...

Young hopefuls, are,
Passionate, with their, effusion.
Dreams of, nirvana,
To circumvent, their confusion.

The bellicoscious, rattle their sabers,
Resort to deeds of blood.
Our reputedly, "venerable leaders",
Now, oxymoron's, bring the red flood

The time of, each beloved,
Comes and passes by.
Few, leave, unwearied and unwounded,
When, quiescence is nigh.

Nevertheless, the halcyon, soothes,
And blitheness ensues, exaltation.
Levity used, to smooth the bruised,
The human spirit, leads, to adaptation.

We all, avoiding, infinite damnation.
Within each tragedy, a coruscation.

SAKURA

People journey, from afar,
For one thing, to behold.
The flowering of, the sakura,
At the close of winter's cold.

From April, betimes,
To, foregoing days of May,
Cherry blossoms, simply sublime,
No one, gazes in wae.

Their blooming, announces,
The advent of spring,
More elegant, than a girl's, flounces.

Delicate pink puffs, of,
Ephemeralness.
Within, the song, of a chough.

They sprout, from black,
Weaved web.
No need for, the claque,
As each shines, like Deneb.

They flock, in their thousands,
And converge, beneath their limbs.
A festival, of legend,
They honour, the coming spring.

O cherry blossoms of pale,
Of your splendour, we regale.

THE PAUPER'S LOR

What is class?
A slap in the face?
An underhanded dig with glass?

How does one, rise through the ranks?
How does one, fall from grace?
The hoi polloi, burdened by their ankhs,
Kneel before, the subbase.

The ambitious, alive, to opportunity,
Might and main, in pain.
They sweat and strain after, in disunity,
Strive, enchained, to obtain.

Pugilists pummel, jostle and hit,
Struggle, scratch, bite and kick.
Each trying, to attain success,
And all which goes with material excess.

Will the paupers, forevermore,
Fill and content the well-to-do?
Shall the bloated, continue,
To keep them in a williwaw?

Looked down upon from miradors,
Fed upon by carnivores.

DILEMMA

Is it possible-
To capture her,
To own her beauty?

Should I chase-
Her grace,
Her uniquity?

May I-
Trap her essence, and,
Will she acquiesce?

If I-
Take her,
Will I break her?

If she-
Gives herself to me,
Will she one day break free?

Conditionally-
If I love thee,
Will you love me?

Am I-
Worthy?
Is she considering me?

Are you weighing the pros and cons in your mind?
Are you pondering the right and wrong kind?

Should I just look from afar?
Am I doomed, to be forever scarred?

Crisis/Opportunity

Spiraling, spiralling, falling down,
My heart is thumping,
My nerves tightly wound.

Dark clouds follow,
Everywhere I roam.
Struggling to traverse,
The warrens I call home.

A charm of finches,
Dart overhead.
Me in the gutter,
I dream of my bed.

Intimates I have loved,
But mostly lost.
I've searched in vain,
And worn the cost.

Where do I find pleasure?
Near naught dear to me.
How do I shake,
This terrible disease?

Now only the merest,
Of vices suffice.
The touch of her hand,
Her smiles entice.

Music I find,
My life's symphony.
My kin and my hopes,
Elegant poetry.

PINING SOUL

When will she come for me?
Will I feel that touch of heaven?
Feelings reach out and find,
Nothing to hold on to
They pass by,
One after another,
Aphrodites
Everyone's but not mine
Angels of the Devil,
Seemingly,
Torture me
No connections, to,
Spread roots, for,
Flowers to spring
Seeds to grow
They do not fall
So many, yet,
None
Will my earth
Dry up and,
Crack?
Without that river,
To nourish my soul
Will the winds of time,
Erode my clock?
Only the seasons
Will tell.

TOGETHER APART

A space cadet looms
As we plummet to our doom
High, so high
And the end is nigh
What will is wrote
In order to denote
He makes himself be
By order and decree
Will the pipe be followed?
For a better tomorrow
Does it matter not?
As we will all rot?
Blood and body of those opposed
Will together, decompose
To fertilize our green earth
Do you see our worth?
Lessons learned or simply rebirth?
Make my brothers and sisters, one
Friends and lovers, all may come
I want for more of a different view
What need for colours, lines and pews?
When sent is spent, wake me up
Storms in teacups all need dup
Why what's seen, is through walls
Is a shame, on us all
So some strive, yet some dive
In the end, we end up rive.

New-Age Sage

Don't seek that way
That way is decay
Not search and destroy
But the search does destroy
You don't need to be trained
Taught and reigned
Let your worries fall
Break down those walls
No truths will you find
To ease load bearing minds
Masters of doctrines
Distort and spin with their din
Folly to follow
Ideas made hollow
When seen not through forefathers
The source becomes larger
If you question your part
Hold on to your heart
Inside you will find
Your link to mankind.

Now, Then And Again

Pictures in my head
As I lay down in my bed
Make chaos in my mind
Looking back far behind
To how it once was then
If only then I had ken
I may have changed my fate
To retaliate without hate
Would I now be who I am?
Would I not give a damn?
Do all paths lead to one place?
Or am I floating around in space?
No one seems to know
So today I'll just follow,
Courage
Nothing left to discourage
If I don't get what I want
I'll still be piedmont
Words come and go
I'll remember them tomorrow
They do not even matter
But still we all get fatter
From stardust, to flesh, to ash
It is pointless to fash
Life is here and now
And then you take your bow.

DARKNESS

Scour the recesses of your black hole
Find your mind is not connected to a soul
Scratching and tearing my inner being
They scan your plan and go sightseeing

In the darkness shadows lurk
Incessant taunting makes you berserk
Fear the self you do not know
In-between you swing down low
Labels make what labels fake
No one cares for pain's mistake

Green inside and blue hangs you
Sights and sounds are yours to choose
Flowers given, smell so sweet
But wilt and die and make you weep
These thunder clouds, are all dark
No silver lining, no more larks

Those who know, stare into space
Although no glow, I put on my face
A barren desert looks in your eye
You brood back and question, why?
Your mood confused, never enthused
Bleak, wills weak, a constant ruse

Spread despair with a touch
Too easy to say, "it don't matter much"
But if you spiral without a fuss
All you'll be is a pile of dust.

THE SKY IS STILL BLUE

As the days go by
I learn again to smile
Even if it's not me
Soon it will be

Always riding the waves
Neuroleptics save
That is what they espouse
But still I hear that rouse
Sweep them to the side
Or confront, do not hide
Round and round and round again
Stay the cycle with mindful Zen

Time sweeps through
Flesh, and bone too
My mind is young but my soul is old
Our spirits have traveled the planes, then they've been sold

I've been left bereft
A lifetime of theft
Still more to come
Will it leave me numb?
Only twenty-six years
Have filled me with fears

Yet you find that you're strong
And life can go on
The sky is still blue
I'll find one who's true
Move toward the day
When I need not be afraid.

Edge Of A Knife

It's hard for me
To do it easy
Or find my fire
Though some inspire

Wasting my time
The time of my prime
Will this disease cease?
So I can find peace

My wishes in life
At the edge of a knife
It's said that it's rife
That's when you're in strife

Rise from my knees
Then I'll be free
Esteem is no dream
May I be redeemed

Feeling my way
Into the sun's rays
It's not my fault
I know I'm no dolt

There are those who are kind
Turn my years to rewind
I've learnt what I've earned
Many times I've been burnt

Still I manage to carry on
A bittersweet soulful song
This time tomorrow I'll envy me
And not the people I used to see.

Forever Let Us Meet

All I need is roses and romance
To our own private symphony, we shall dance
An intoxicating fragrance, her scent and breath mingles
Her kiss, sublime bliss, the memory lingers

From Monday to Sunday, all I dream of is her
Last night we embraced, I wish we always were
Together we share, the night sky's full moon
The stars are ours, Paris in June

You and I, defy, misery
Partners so perfect, like Adam and Eve
I want to immerse myself, in your good grace
And spend my life staring, at your sweet face

In the past, I know, you've cradled my soul
And how you've told, you'll always do so

Please call me your love
A love sent from above
If I could sing, I would croon
A ballad to you

As I make you my wife
For the rest of my life
Even though they disagree
We'll be for eternity

You won me over from the start
With the generosity of your heart
My soul mate, you are my hope
Without you, I would not cope
From there to despair
There would be nothing for I would care

So, my complete
Forever, let us meet
If you stay with me
I'll make you happy.

Please Don't Refuse

Please babe, will you listen
You know I'd never go dis'in
If apart, don't deny we'd be missing
I just want us to be kissing

Wait lady, before you go
There's something I think you ought to know
I wasn't brave enough to let it show
Everything I am, to you, I owe

Angel girl there's only you, there's no confusion
All those others are just an illusion
We can't accept any intrusion
Let's take it to the final conclusion

So honey, don't walk away from us
There's more to us than physical lust
We have to, rebuild the trust
With time, I know, we'll readjust

Well, my darling, what do you choose?
Will you stay with me or will you move?
Leave and surely we'll both lose
This is my plea, please don't refuse

Soon, sweet thing, we'll forget the past
What will happen next, I can't forecast
But I know, our love is vast
And I'll stay with you until my last.

DISMANTLED

What happened to the
Joyous times
When turns in kind were
The norm
Above all else
I was surrounded
With
Mother's love
Father's protection
Brother's affinity
Extended community who
Kept within
Their bosom
All of us
Their children

Separation anxiety
Is the order
Of the day
Today
Disconnected
Detached
Disenchanted
Dislocated
Disinfected
Dismayed

Even he
A wall between
Within walls
So tall

So wide
So thick
Can it be dismantled?
Like the wall
Between east and west

Maybe
I am that wall
Take it apart
Take apart me
To a degree
Would that be better for me?
Useful to the
Useless
Nature is merciless

All grow
Except me
Phase by phase
Release me
To the next stage
I've been here
Too long

Avant-garde
I wish I was
Instead
I regress
Find it hard to
Address
The nightmares in my mind
Horrors of my own creation
Why can't they be benign?

Transcendence
Is it possible?
Independence
From the hospital.

OF SHOOTING STARS

Take your fibre
For intestinal fortitude
Cut the wires
Join the multitude

From the drought
Rivers run dry
Bring rains about
Where birds fly

Tattooed onto my face
Stress from the years of waste
Remove it, leave no trace
Take comfort in her grace

Find sunlight in the
Darkest corner
Traverse wide and far
Don't be a mourner

From deepest wounds
Come smoothest scars
Inspire sweet tunes
Of shooting stars

Of shooting stars
They never last
Bright and stark
A human task.

FALLEN

How can those who
Respected him so
And held him in
Such high regard and
Esteem
Treat him like......?

I guess I'm partly at fault
An undeserving result
Not the mighty
But fallen frightly

He who led
Commanded those
In his stead
Void and holes

Emperor of
The lost souls
Now not though
Lost control

Even once strong mind
Has turned inside
From a whim
Deserted him

A cause lost
Human dross
Shame to speak
Of the weak

Could not depend
On ties to mend
Fractured reality
Or inject insanity

So head is layed
Upon bed made
Of broken innocence
And self-destructiveness
Is that all?
For him, once tall
Passing moments
A life of lament.

DECAY

When in doubt
Delude yourself
Wish away
Mouth decay

Interlude
Attitude
Forget the crude

Relief in sight
Away with spite
Water the seeds
Fertilize the soil
Drink the mead
From your toil
Feast like royals

Back to the play
Play it out today
Day after day
Cannot escape
My own rape

Pillage and plunder
Through the sunder
Your own brain
Brain of bane

Head of state
All too late
Lobotomize
My own demise

Gathered moss
A life of chaos
Both my and their loss
Via con Dios.

SILENT TESTIMONY

Sit at the back
Do not speak
Hide the tracks
Be the freak

Flee the scene
Into retreat
Silent feet
Without dreams

Way is paved
By lost days
Filtered rays
Lunacy reigns

Set my face
To commonplace
At her base
No interface

The anti-life
Consciousness
Less interest
To afterlife

My self-loathing
Keeps downtrodden
Endure while rotting
From nothing something.

MOMENTS

Moments
Where are my moments?
A first exhilarating kiss
Of passionate lovers, to be promiscuous
Shared feelings
Memories of union
Contentedness
Bright, bubbling, summer days
Lounging and playing in sun's rays
Bleak winters, together warming
Autumn dreary, leaves falling
Spring, breaking through
Hearts hopes, anew
Wanting
Being wanted
Needing
Being needed
Uninhibited with her
Journeys of expansion
A deluge of romanticism
Senses overlapping
Life trapping
Express!
No regress
Spreading myself
Until I engulf
The earth
Black holes
Inside

Filled up by the world
Is that too much to,
Expect?
Life free from inaction's,
Regret.

TRACES

Je ne oublier nien
Words
Cutting
Memories burning
Life smashing
Breaking
Breaking down
Fractured
Dysfunctionalised
A broken mirror
Falling to hundreds of little,
Pieces
Creases,
In my mind
Suffocation
Going blind
So I cannot see
Even splintered me
Disappear in the deluge
Find a place to take refuge
Thunder stalks the sky
Lightning creeps behind
Coming in from the cold
Look for traces
Of I, of old.

MINE

Depression
The succession
Buy your blues away
Drink to make them stay
I think what I think
It never changes
Pull me back from the brink
Help rearrange us
Of what dreams I hold
Could not be foretold
Oh why, oh why, I ask?
Do I cry for this task?
Matters that do not matter
Shatter, they always shatter
He said "Nothings trivial"
I find it believable
Unbelievably believable
My life, trivial?
A wind in my sails,
At the edge of the world
I hope not to fail,
In position I'm curled
When the balance is equal,
Left and right
There will be no more reasons,
Left to fight
Except to hold onto
The lives on the line
Accept there are those who
Will be only mine.

Ode To Edgar 1

Once, I woke
Stark the note
A shadow I saw
Against the wall
Straight up, I sat
Flew past, a bat
Again, the note
Lump in, my throat
Racing, my pulse
My courage, false
Crept out of bed
Whirling, my head
Attached to the dark
My mind, did lark
Eyes, a searching
Hoped for, an urchin
By the windows,
Of my door
Please rescind, oh
My poor lor.

Ode To Edgar 2

Then, again, the note
Searched for, my tote
A rustle, I heard
A tussle, I feared
Only, the half moon
Stood out in the gloom
Threw shadows across
My room, I was lost
Within, mine own fears
With my ears, could not hear
Anything, now more
Outside the door
Felt for the switch
But found a glitch
No illumination
To kill contemplation
Of demons in darkness
Surroundings of starkness.

Ode To Edgar 3

Thinking, what should I do?
Slowly began to move
Adjusting to dark
That stalker, that shark
I felt in the room
My impending doom
Now, a creaking
Of footsteps, speaking
To my mortal core
Foreboding, I bore
Thoughts and images
Raced through my head
Of monsters and killers
Under my bed
My heart, a flutter
My hands, like butter
A chill in my spine
Upon my fears, it dined.

Ode To Edgar 4

Now frozen in place
I tried hard to trace
The source of my fears
It must be near
Something loomed
My home, my tomb
Awaiting the drop
Could do nothing to stop
Then, a bell went
I woke sweating and spent
'Twas a mere nightmare
Ne're was I so fright scared
I breathed with relief
My mind, my courage thief
I wiped sweat from my brow
Time to start the day now
I raised my tired body
Felt unrested and shoddy
And then…..there was a note…..

BANE

I hate him, I hate him, so fucking much!
That bastard he has, no bloody touch!
His sense empty, since he was born,
His pride and ego is all that he mourns;
He talks at me, talks at me, as though I'm a child,
My anger boils over; I can taste the bile;
When will he give up on being top dog?
I'd like to put him in a vice and tighten the cogs;
Smash his teeth, and break his nose,
At his funeral there will be not a rose,
From me, from me,
His taunting face is all I can see;
Not for him, will I let it slide,
Would he be sorry, if I had died?
Wrestle those claws, out of my back,
Strain on the chains, make them crack,
Fight those demons, with all of my might,
Unburden myself and then just take flight;
Yet still he tries, to hammer me down,
I tell him "get fucked!" He repeats with a frown;
My self-respect, he wants to supplant,
Until all that I do is rant, rant, rant!
Slowly I fall, farther from grace,
If his brain had features, dumbfounded its face;
I spiral, spiral, further insane,
I hate him, I hate him, his ego my bane!

PIERCING BLUE

She is the one, my thoughts and dreams,
My heart's queen, for her I scream;
To all I must, confess and discuss
My love for her, my enduring lust;

I cry for loneliness, and yearn at night
For not being with her, not holding her tight,
I lie in my bed, head against the wall,
Her on the other side, oh to knock on her door,

She gives me a glimpse and teases me,
With the almighty, I pray and plea;
Is she the angel who will redeem my soul?
To make our connection, make me whole

Her so beautiful, eyes of piercing blue,
She makes me full, Lord give me a clue!

HARBINGERS

Dusk,
The sun has hidden itself away,
The moon crept up into its place;
Birds no longer sing and play,
Their fluttering replaced by their
Leather winged counterparts,
Sightless harbingers usher in night,
How eerily they negotiate the rooftops
And grasping branches they make home; and the
Chill shrieking of their calls, as they
Tussle with other creatures of darkness;
Muted wings flap deafeningly with
Foreboding;
And one after another, then in twos
And threes, more, they come
Seemingly to take my soul,
Wishing they would, I await them,
But time and again just pass by,
Bringing the small hours and solitude with
Them;
And I await
For something, but nothing;
What has awakened them and drawn their
Black presence forth?
These dark wind-riders,
A primal force breaking through each
Grim exterior, reverberating in minds
So blank and bleak, hollow for their evil;
Rising from nowhere and disappearing into

Shadows,
Time and again coming into vision and vanish,
Spellbinding, mythical demons in flight;
What ghastly mission do they hold?
I await...

THE WANDERER'S EYE

By the final throes, of breath
Of night, breathing its last breath,
The wanderer had come upon her,
And glimpsed among the animal furs;
Hours just passed, now past,
Majestic features only Olympus surpassed,
Not just wandering body, but wandering orb,
He thought to himself, this one I adore;
Bathing herself, in the placid blue,
Voyeur a sudden, the filthy man grew;
Feeling a presence, she viewed his intrusion,
Startled and wet, all the more her confusion;
Gathering her senses, the Lady decided,
For flatteries sake, she would abide it;
"Come thither thou" escaped her lips,
Hastily, he came to grips;
By chance, upon fairest maiden,
He beat cobwebs, fully laden;
For no opportunity missed, he sprung forth,
In impatience o'er breech, opposite north,
In arrow's desire and silver-backed grasp,
Stung repeatedly, of speedy wasp;
With sensibilities, didst she protest
This fumbling, lusting one, who did molest,
And with that, a lonesome passerby,
Did hear the complaints, and did eye,
Being of gentlemanly demeanour
And offended more, for his seeing her,
Took his blade unto the sky,
Observing this, the invader did cry
"Come thither, I heard spoke",

Caused pause, to revoke,
The curtain call, from the plunge,
And later, the saviour would have expunged
From coil, not snake, but snake did sense
A swift, cold blow, so did repent,
For that, did cause a turtle to shrink,
Pleaded innocence, for time to think;
But innocence broken, proved by sight,
Bore confrontation and begged a fight;
"Durst ye pretend, to not offend
Virtue of this, fair maiden friend?"
The gentleman stood poised, for reply,
"T'was her proposition, mercy, beg I",
Fumbling with his buckle, and upon his knees;
"Do away with your sword, good sir, please!"
The maiden cried foul, "he is a beast!"
"Dear maiden, no, you are a tease!"
Trapped and unarmed, the wanderer raced
Only in thought, he was stuck in this place,
For gentle heart, the nobleman's dilemma:
"What be your name?" The maiden replied "Emma",
"How would you have me, deal with this man?"
"So he always remembers, cut off his hands!"
The wanderer cried "no! Carpentry be my trade!"
He leapt and he yelled "someone give me aid!"
"Her beauty in moonlight drove my mind to distraction,
"Sir, you are a man, do you deny her attraction?"
"Question my morals, should ye dare not!
For this is one matter, which will make me hot!"
In red rush only, not under the collar,
The scoundrel offered bribes, but he'd take not a dollar;
By destiny, this knight, had once been betrothed
Though before he married, she was lost to a rogue,
With these wounds, to his mind, brought anew,

His thoughts became vengeance, upon this poor fool:
"Prepare thyself, for almighty judgement!"
But the wanderer, merely, held up a parchment;
Fearing the inevitable, though too ashamed before
He screamed "I'm the King's messenger, kill me, break the law!"
Once more the noble knight pulled back from the brink,
At last the man had found, the knight's armour's chink;
As only the King, may decide his messenger's fate,
Knowing his position, the knight's vengeance, too late,
Grimacing in anger, then suddenly pain,
The knight's face was ashen, for he was slain
By arrow aimed, and meeting its target,
Of guard, in accompaniment, to the messenger's legate;
Holding his sword, to King's messenger, none
May do so with impunity, it brought him undone;
Upon seeing his fate, the maiden took flight,
And jumped in the lake, swimming for all might,
But, alas, she could not, and promptly drowned,
The rest shrugged their shoulders, barely a frown;
They took to their steeds, horses built
For distance. The messenger alone with his guilt.
Now the knight's spirit haunts the dark woods,
The maiden trapped in the lake, crying for her girlhood.

A FRACTURED MIRROR REFLECTS ALL BUT NOT ONE

What tiger without teeth
Knew he was a hunter?
A fractured mirror,
I saw him, I saw me

The moon reflected the sun
But only so far
A broken reality
I saw him, I saw me undone

Stars shine on down
But died long ago
Driving winds cut through rock
Bringing misery and woe

Atoms only split
When you overload
Like the levees of your mind
When you travel down that road

The virgin just wants one
A junky wants just one more
The assassin makes no selection
And suicide is against the law

Only as intelligent as I need to be
But never needing to be smart
How do you know who you are,
When you know not what you art?

Writers invent character
Though reveal their own minds
The figments do pretend, yet
Are at odds with their own kind

When she wanted me all
I refused to give
Now I have nothing to give
I need a soft place to fall

Only irony decides who's won
Because there's no other way
Black and white become grey
I saw me not as one.

Deja-Vu

Time was, in one's time,
What was done then
Is done now,
Always for the first time,
As time elapses, slowly,
Steadily, without waver,
And urgency is impressed;
For yesterday's battle, is
Today's war. A gathering.
And everything changes, but
Nothing is gained.
Independence is inexplicably linked,
Attached
Self-involving, yet omniscient.
As lines deepen, recognition disappears
Into simplicity. Raw and primal.
Demons are the definers,
Diligent in their connections,
But always just beyond reach.
Guilt does not disappear along with
Conscience.
Bound to the subconscious.
Language is staked through the heart.
Glorious and terrible in piety's
Chains. Broken only by swords hand forged in
Steel. Heated, pounded, and folded upon itself.
Exacting every layer, and
Tempered by will's desire.
Linkages in karma are
Its own strength and weakness at once.
The discerning being makes note.

SANITARIUM

The winter was cold,
in the old sanitarium.
But our hero was bold,
and nothing would bother him.
He banged on the door,
heard echoes then silence.
The halls betrayed none,
of its mayhem and violence.
Then footsteps approached,
first one, two and three.
The door clanged open,
quick, it's now time to flee.
He burst through the soldiers,
ran down the corridor.
But ahead only bars,
he could go further no more.
The white coats came charging,
needle in hand.
When would they ever,
learn to understand.
That he was an eagle,
ready to soar.
Shot down and defeathered,
chained to the floor.
Out came the jacket,
he went kicking and screaming.
Dragged back to his cell,
to stare at the ceiling.
The door clanged shut,
the footsteps disappeared.
His boldness was gone,

now only afeared.
He dreamed of his lady,
whom he never would see.
In here only shadows,
doomed to never be free.

Union

My love is my lord
Not the Lord but my love
Each must cast out to reel in that one
A mind which finds is what I crave
A path of purity I want to pave
When eyes of mine meet hers in reverse
I feel it lifting, melting my curse
She floats among the milieu, comes my way
The scent of perfume, I cannot stray
Lips spread wide, a smile made just for me
Her essence, so precious, our chemistry
A joke, my heart floats, in ecstasy
Each meeting, each moment, what intensity
Expectation soars, harbours elation
Dazed and bewitched by her incantation
Food for the soul, is my starving at an end
We open ourselves, no need to pretend
Be mine tonight, and forever more
I'll love you always, and I will be yours.

FLOW

People are rarely what they are
They fade, change and collect scars
From moment to moment, one thing to another
Life is ever changing, each day to discover
Each day I send out to receive different news
In turn they come back with different views
Beware to take care of knives eyes
With aim without frame behind smiles lies
We gather in arms at the hour of mirth
Don't wear out open doors or your worth
Judgement without reason brings misunderstanding
Keeps each half apart and freestanding
How can it be so that to know is to love?
When all I think is my personalities not enough
Sometimes we all need a memory enema
To forget our regrets, heel scars forever
Desires passion burns bright then lights out
While love simmers and lingers, sprouts wings without doubt
When hurt creeps in, our years desert us
Explain the pain then leave it we must
Should we see what we deal with jaded eyes?
Child's mind we cannot find as we become wise
Though wise is all lies, within no truth
Given up on surprise, that day you will rue
Gaze into the maze, see a fragile reflection
A dire inquire urges further introspection
Make no mistake, she stands without hands
And so must you for your horizons to expand
Tune your ears to unfamiliar sounds
You'll know something special when it comes around
I often ponder and conclude, mine's not to share

Sleeping in my bed the other side lays bare
Earth rotates around the sun as it spins on its axis
As do our thoughts, troubles which tax us
Descend on impending thoughts of despair
Close down those avenues, make them rare
Let torment ride on winds which blow
Let pain change to circumstance, and finally, flow.

POETRY The Four Lives by Nicholas Pak is the culmination of many years writing by the author.

His intention was to write a book of poetry, and he spent approximately twenty years writing and rewriting, until he was satisfied with the standard of the prose.

Sadly, he passed away, before his idea could be realised.

His family decided to continue with his plan, collecting his work and submitting it for publication.

Be prepared for a roller coaster of emotion as you read each poem. Ranging from thoughtful, to romantic to humorous and at times, full of despair, the author has observed or experienced all as he looked for inspiration to write the book.

Eagles Nest 2015
Photo by Colleen Marshall

About the Author

Nicholas Pak was an avid reader and loved the English language. His poetry can sometimes be a bit dark, often has a humorous twist. Whilst some of his poetry sensitively expresses emotions and relationships, each poem tells a story, that the reader can visualize a picture.

Nick lived in Melbourne for his first 22 years, then moved to Sydney to live with his father, who had relocated for work, and where Nick subsequently died.

Nick had attempted tertiary level studies but had to defer due to health issues, therefore not completing his degree. He passed away aged 38 years before he could complete the publishing process. His mother, Colleen Marshall is publishing this poetry book on his behalf.

Printed in the United States
By Bookmasters